C000005467

alaskan malamute

understanding and
caring for your breed

Written by
Michael James

alaskan malamute

understanding and
caring for your breed

Written by
Michael James

Pet Book Publishing Company

Bishton Farm, Bishton Lane, Chepstow, NP16 7LG, United Kingdom.
881 Harmony Road, Unit A, Eatonton, GA31024 United States of America.

Printed and bound in China through Printworks International.

Every reasonable care has been taken in the compilation of this
publication. The Publisher and Author cannot accept liability for any
loss, damage, injury or death resulting from the keeping of Alaskan
Malamutes by user(s) of this publication, or from the use of any
materials, equipment, methods or information recommended in this
publication or from any errors or omissions that may be found in the
text of this publication or that may occur at a future date, except as
expressly provided by law.

The 'he' pronoun is used throughout this book instead of the rather
impersonal 'it', however no gender bias is intended.

ISBN: 978-1-906305-80-2
ISBN: 1-906305-80-3

Acknowledgements

The publishers would like to thank the following for help with
photography: Tracy Morgan Animal Photography
(www.animalphotographer.co.uk); Andrea and Mark Blackburn; Mike
and Chris John (Cristakell).

Contents

Introducing the Alaskan Malamute

The Alaskan Malamute is among the most stunning of all dog breeds. Strong and powerful, he shows a striking resemblance to the wolf, but is clothed in the most magnificent coat, designed to withstand the extreme temperatures of his Arctic home.

The Alaskan Malamute has been our helpmate for thousands of years, but it is only relatively recently that we welcomed him into our homes as a companion dog.

Bred to pull heavy loads in the frozen wastes of the Arctic, the Malamute has always been valued, first and foremost, as a working dog. He is still used as a freight dog in his native home, but with the advent of

sled racing and other related sports, he has been the breed of choice for many who want to compete. The Mal is not as swift as the Siberian Husky; his ability lies in his tremendous strength and endurance, which allow him to cover long distances, pulling heavy loads in the worst conditions.

The number of Malamutes exhibited in the show ring has always been relatively few, and registrations of puppies reflected this low level interest in the breed. However, in the last decade, the picture has changed dramatically and the Malamute has soared in popularity; registrations in the UK have increased ten-fold.

It is hard to give reasons for this change in attitude, but there is no doubt that the Alaskan Malamute has found a new role as an outstanding companion dog.

The right choice

Given the fact that the Alaskan Malamute was bred to live in sub-zero temperatures and work all day pulling heavy loads, he has adapted surprisingly well to his life as a pet dog. However, he can be challenging, and prospective owners need to weigh up the pros and cons before deciding that this is their breed of choice.

Pros

- Beautiful to look at.

- Superb temperament – loyal and affectionate.

- Good with children.

- Highly trainable.

- The coat is odor-free

Cons

- A strong prey drive means he cannot be trusted around small animals and other livestock.

- The instinct to chase is too strong to allow free running exercise.

- Can be aggressive with other dogs.

- Tends to be assertive, particularly if he has an owner he does not respect.

- Dog hair – it gets everywhere!

If the pros outweigh the cons, you will find the Alaskan Malamute a loyal and trustworthy member of your family, and you will never regret your choice. But if you have any concerns that this breed may be too much for you and your family, or he may not fit into your lifestyle, you are strongly advised to think again.

Tracing back in time

The Alaskan Malamute has a history stretching back some 3,000 years. Throughout that time he has been of service to man, working tirelessly in the most severe conditions.

All our dogs are descended from the wolf, and when you look at an Alaskan Malamute, the resemblance is striking. It is thought that the breeds we term as Nordic sled dogs, which include the Alaskan Malamute, American Eskimo Dog, the Siberian Husky and the Samoyed, are descended from the Arctic wolf – a snow white wolf that can still be found in the Canadian Arctic.

The breed we know as the Alaskan Malamute gets its name from the Mahlemuit Eskimos of Alaska. To begin with the dogs were used to help with the hunt, tackling animals as big as bears and also using their sense of smell to locate the blowholes of seals. When the hunt was over, the Malamutes took on an additional task, dragging heavy carcasses back to the home base.

As time went on, the Eskimos increasingly used their dogs as a mean of transport, choosing the strongest and most powerful to pull sleds loaded

The Siberian Husky shares similar roots to the Alaskan Malamute.

with food and supplies. Alaskan Malamutes are solidly built and are not as fast as the Siberian Husky, but they more than made up for this with their tenacity and their ability to work in the harshest of conditions. The Eskimo people found these dogs surprisingly biddable; they could be trained to work as a team, and showed great loyalty to their human taskmasters.

The Gold Rush

In 1896 gold was discovered in Klondike, and suddenly one of the harshest and most inhospitable parts of the world was flooded with people eager to cash in on the new-found wealth in Alaska.

The adventurers encountered many difficulties, and finding a means of transport proved a major issue. Materials were needed to build the mines, to ferry workers to them, to bring in food supplies and other provisions, and finally to transport the gold away from the mines.

The answer was to use dog teams. The Alaskan Malamute with his remarkable strength, his dense coat, his thick pads designed for snow travel, and his ability to keep going for long distances, was the perfect choice.

In 1908 Jackson B. Corbett wrote:

...a Malamute is the most cheerful worker and the most obstinate shirk, intelligent or dense, but always cunning, crafty and wise; stealing anything not tied down. He makes an exceptionally strong and reliable leader in that place, displaying the cunning, wisdom and trickery that characterize the breed.

There are probably more than a few Malamute owners today that recognize these traits in their dogs...

Cunning, wisdom and trickery – the hallmarks of the breed...

Developing
the breed

With the advent of the Gold Rush at the end of the 19th century the demand for sled dogs was so great that other breeds were brought in and were interbred with the local sled dogs.

This spelt disaster for the Alaskan Malamute, and the purity of the breed was nearly destroyed. Fortunately, the Mahlemuit Eskimos continued to live in relative isolation and so they retained a gene pool of purebred Alaskan Malamutes.

Expedition dogs

The early part of the 20th century was a time of polar exploration and, once again, the Alaskan Malamute was the breed of choice for transporting supplies.

In 1909 Malamutes were used on the rival teams of Commander Robert Peary and Dr Frederick Cook who battled to be the first to reach the North Pole.

Malamutes later accompanied Admiral Richard Byrd on his two expeditions to Antarctica – in 1928-1930 and 1933-1935 – sometimes at great cost. In Little America, Antarctica, there is plaque erected in memory of all the dogs who lost their lives during these years.

The great mercy race

In 1925 Alaskan Malamutes, along with Siberian Huskies, were crucial in saving the villagers of Nome on the Seward peninsula in Alaska.

A radio message was received stating that there was an outbreak of diphtheria, a highly contagious and often fatal disease and supplies of serum were dwindling. Anchorage – over 600 miles away – was the nearest source of supply. The route was treacherous and could only be traveled by sled dogs. It took the very best mushers a month to cover the distance.

This was start of the most amazing relay race of all time. Battling through the worst of conditions, with temperatures dropping to minus 30 degrees and winds reaching 40 miles an hour, the serum was taken cross-country by teams of sled dogs. Siberian Huskies had the edge where speed was concerned, but the big-hearted Alaskan Malamute was tireless in this race against time.

Finally they made it to Nome and the serum arrived in time to save the village. The sled dog teams had covered the 674-mile journey in 27 and half hours – a world record.

A statue was erected to honor the heroic sled dogs in New York's Central Park, and the inscription reads:

Dedicated to the indomitable spirit of the sled dogs that relayed antitoxin 600 miles over rough ice, treacherous waters; through Arctic blizzard from Nenana to the relief of the stricken Nome in the winter of 1925.

Endurance – Fidelity – Intelligence.

The Malamute today

The American Kennel Club gave official breed recognition to the Alaskan Malamute in 1935, and for many decades the Malamute remained very much a specialist dog. He was used for search and rescue during both World Wars, and is still highly valued in this role today. He is also prized by sports competitors; long distance sled racing is now an international sport and is highly competitive at the top level.

In recent times, the Malamute has become increasingly popular as a companion dog, and numbers have increased dramatically, particularly in the UK.

Families are drawn to this remarkably handsome dog, with his strong, independent character and his loyal, affectionate nature. However, the Alaskan Malamute is first and foremost a working dog; he needs an active lifestyle and an owner who understands him.

What should an Alaskan Malamute look like?

The majestic Alaskan Malamute draws admiring glances wherever he goes with his dignified bearing and rugged good looks. So what makes a Malamute so special?

The aim of breeders is to produce dogs that are sound healthy, typical examples of their chosen breed, in terms of both looks and temperament. To achieve this, they are guided by a Breed Standard, which is a written blueprint describing what the perfect specimen should look like.

Of course, there is no such thing as a 'perfect' dog, but breeders aspire to produce dogs that conform as closely as possible to the picture in words presented by the Breed Standard. In the show ring, judges use the Breed Standard to assess the dogs that come before

them, and it is the dog that, in their opinion, comes closest to the ideal, that will win top honors.

This has significance beyond the sport of showing for it is the dogs that win in the ring that will be used for breeding. The winners of today are therefore responsible for passing on their genes to future generations and preserving the breed in its best form.

There are some differences in the wording of the Breed Standard depending on national kennel clubs; the American Standard is certainly more descriptive than the English version and gives you a better idea of what the breed should really look like.

General appearance

The Alaskan Malamute is built for strength and endurance and the overriding impression should be of power. He is heavy boned and, according to the American Standard, "stands well over his pads" which gives an appearance of much activity and a proud carriage.

Temperament

This is an affectionate and friendly dog, and despite his loyalty and devotion, he is not a "one man" dog. He can be playful, but a sense of dignity in mature Malamutes is a hallmark of the breed.

Points of anatomy

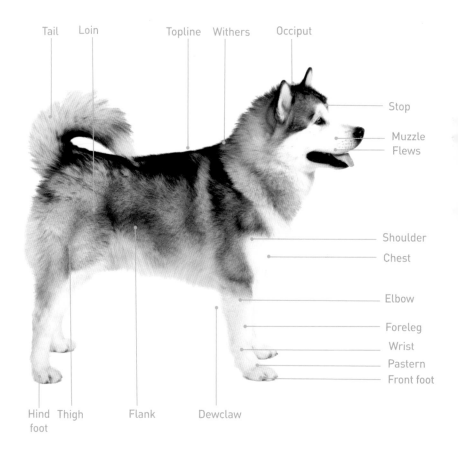

Tail

Loin

Topline

Withers

Occiput

Stop

Muzzle

Flews

Shoulder

Chest

Elbow

Foreleg

Wrist

Pastern

Front foot

Hind foot

Thigh

Flank

Dewclaw

Head and skull

The head is broad and powerful, but should never appear coarse. The skull is broad, rounded between the ears, gradually narrowing and flattening as it reaches the eyes. The stop (the step between the muzzle and the foreface) is slight but perceptible. The muzzle is large in proportion to the size of the skull, scarcely diminishing in width or depth from the stop.

The pigment on the nose, lips and eye rims is black, except in red dogs where it is brown. A pink-streaked 'snow nose' – where the pigment changes color in winter – is acceptable.

Eyes

The eyes are almond-shaped and set obliquely in the skull. The American Standard asks for medium-sized eyes, whereas the UK Standard describes them as "moderately large". However, both Standards agree that dark eyes are preferred. Blue eyes, which are commonly seen in the Siberian Husky, are considered highly undesirable. In fact, the American Standard regards them as a disqualifying fault.

Ears

The ears are small in proportion to the head, and this feature contributes to the unique Malamute look. They are triangular in shape, rounded at the tip and set wide apart on the back edge of the skull. The ears are generally erect and point slightly forward, but when a dog is working they may be folded against the skull.

Mouth

The jaws are broad with large teeth meeting in a scissor bite, where the teeth on the upper jaw closely overlap the teeth on the lower jaw. The lips are close fitting.

Neck

The neck is strong and moderately arched.

Forequarters

The shoulders are moderately sloping; the forelegs are heavily boned and well muscled. It is essential that the legs do not appear short in proportion to the body. The front legs are straight as far as the pasterns. The pasterns (which act as the main shock absorbers) are short and strong; they are "almost straight" when viewed from the side according to the UK Standard, or "slightly sloping" if you go with the American Standard.

Body

The body should convey power and strength. The chest is deep and well developed, and should be approximately half the height of the dog at the shoulders. The back is straight, sloping gently to the hips; the loins are hard and well muscled. The body is compactly built, but should not appear short coupled.

Hindquarters

The hind legs are broad and heavily muscled and should indicate tremendous propelling power. The stifles (the dog's 'knees') are moderately bent, and the hocks (the dog's 'ankles') are broad, strong and also moderately bent. Viewed from behind, the hind legs should be in line with the movement of the front legs.

Feet

The American Standard describes the feet as being "of the snowshoe type". They are large and compact with well-arched toes that have a protective growth of hair between them. The pads are thick and well cushioned.

Tail

The tail is moderately set and follows the line of the spine, curving gently upwards. It is well furred and carried over the back when the dog is working; it should give the appearance of a waving plume.

Gait/movement

On the move, the Malamute is steady, balanced and powerful. The drive comes from the hindquarters which is transmitted to the forequarters with a smooth, reaching stride. Movement should appear easy, tireless and rhythmic.

Coat

The Malamute has a spectacular coat, designed to withstand the Arctic temperatures. The undercoat is dense, wooly and oily and should be 1to 2in (2.5-5cm) in depth. The coarse outer guard hairs form a short to medium length coat along the sides of the body, but it increases in length around the shoulders and neck, down the back, over the rump, with breeching ('trousers') on the hind legs, and a well-plumed tail.

Color

The color ranges from light grey through intermediate shadings to black, sable (gold), and shadings of sable to red, all with white on the underbelly, parts of the feet, and as part of the face markings. The only solid color that is allowed is white.

The markings on the face are cap-like or mask-like, or a combination of both. A white blaze on the forehead, a white collar or spot on the nape are acceptable – the American Standard calls them "attractive and acceptable". Broken colors over the body are undesirable.

Size

The American Standard states that the ideal size for freighting males is 25in (64cm) at the shoulder, with a weight of 85lb (38kg); females should be 23in (58cm) in height, and weigh 75lbs (33kg). The UK Standard gives greater leeway, stipulating 25 to 28in (64-71cm) for males, and 23 to 26in (58-66cm), with a weight guide of 85 to 125lb (38-56kg). However, both Standards agree that consideration of size should not outweigh that of type, proportion or movement.

Summing up

Although the majority of Alaskan Malamutes are kept as pet dogs or working dogs and will never be exhibited in the show ring, it is important that breeders strive for perfection and try to produce dogs that adhere as closely as possible to the Breed Standard. This is the best way of ensuring that the Malamute remains sound in mind and body, and retains the characteristics that are unique to this very special breed.

What do you want from your Malamute?

There are hundreds of dog breeds to choose from, so how can you be sure that the Alaskan Malamute is the right breed for you? Before you take the plunge into Malamute ownership, you need to be 100 per cent confident that this is the breed that is best suited to your lifestyle.

Companion

Throughout his long history, the Alaskan Malamute has been prized for his service to mankind. This is a dog who will give you his all; he is loving and affectionate, but it is his unswerving loyalty that is most treasured.

However, owning a Malamute comes at a price – and you must be very sure that you know what you are taking on. Yes, he is a wonderful family dog, and will get on well with children, given the correct training and socialization. But do you want a large, powerful dog with a strong hunting instinct that cannot be trusted off lead?

This is a very important consideration, as you cannot expect a dog that was bred for long distance endurance to tolerate a home where he never has the opportunity to free run.

Although loving and trustworthy with his family, the Alaskan Malamute does not always take kindly to living with other dogs. If you want more than one dog, you will have to work very hard at supervising early interactions so your Mal understands that he must accept another canine on his patch.

You should also consider the Malamute's coat. Developed to withstand the Arctic winter, he is not ideally suited to a home with carpets and central heating. He will adapt, but beware the coat shedding. Malamutes do shed huge amounts of hair, and if you are house-proud, this may not be the breed for you.

Sports dog

If you are an active, outdoors, sporty person, the Alaskan Malamute could be a great choice. Intelligent and focused, he can be trained to a high standard, and there are a number of canine sports where he excels, particularly those that are designed for sled dogs.

For more information, see Opportunities for Malamutes, page 150.

Show dog

Do you have ambitions to exhibit your Alaskan Malamute in the show ring? This is becoming increasingly popular among Malamute owners, but you do need the right dog to start with.

If you plan to show your Mal, you need to track down a show quality puppy, and train him so he will perform in the show ring, and accept the detailed 'hands on' examination that he will be subjected to when he is being judged.

It is also important to bear in mind that not every puppy with show potential develops into a top-quality specimen, and so you must be prepared to love your Malamute and give him a home for life, even if he doesn't make the grade.

What does your Malamute want from you?

A dog cannot speak for himself, so we need to view the world from a canine perspective and work out what an Alaskan Malamute needs in order to live a happy, contented and fulfilling life.

Time and commitment

First of all, a Malamute needs a commitment that you will care for him for the duration of his life – guiding him through his puppyhood, enjoying his adulthood, and being there for him in his later years. If all potential owners were prepared to make this pledge, there would be scarcely any dogs in rescue.

The Alaskan Malamute was not bred to be a companion dog; this is a role he has adapted to, but it is important

to bear in mind that he retains a strong work ethic. You need to be confident that you can cater for his special needs – giving him the exercise he needs, and providing mental stimulation so that he does not become bored and destructive. If you cannot give your Malamute the time and commitment he deserves, you would be strongly advised to delay owning a dog until your circumstances change.

Practical matters

The Alaskan Malamute has a glorious coat, but you may find it all over your carpets, clothes and furniture! In order to keep the situation under control, you will need to groom your Malamute several times a week, taking time to work right through to the undercoat. Twice a year, a Malamute will 'blow' his coat – and then you really will have your work cut out ... For more information on grooming, see pages 107.

In terms of exercise, a Malamute needs the opportunity to use his body – walking, running, investigating scents, and, ideally, taking part in one of the canine sports. Providing this is not as easy as it sounds as the Malamute's strong prey drive means that he cannot be allowed free running exercise in open spaces. However, he is the ideal choice if you want to get involved in active dog sports such as canicross, agility, and mushing.

If you do not want to get involved in formal dog sports, you can still provide suitable exercise, jogging with your Mal, or training him to run alongside you when you are on a bike. But before you take on a Malamute, you need to think long and hard about how you are going to organize this aspect of his life.

Leadership

The Alaskan Malamute has a strong will and an independent nature, which is not always conducive to pet ownership. If a Mal does not have an owner he respects, he can become assertive, and you will find that he is ruling the roost.

Training and socialization are key ingredients in creating a dog that is content with his role in the family and is able to cope with the stresses of modern life. He also needs mental stimulation to channel his energies in a positive way. Deviant and inappropriate behavior are very often the result of boredom; a clever dog that has nothing to do will quickly find his own agenda.

The Alaskan Malamute may not be the best breed for a first-time owner. An understanding of dog behavior and a real interest in training should be considered essential if you want to take on this magnificent, but challenging breed.

Extra considerations

Now you have decided that an Alaskan Malamute is the dog of your dreams, you can narrow your choice so you know exactly what you are looking for.

Male or female?

The choice of whether you get a male or female Malamute comes down to personal preference. There is not much difference in temperament; both are loving and loyal and adapt well to family life. Both have a strong independent streak, but males may be slightly more assertive, particularly during adolescence.

From a practical point of view, the male is a bigger, heavier animal, and this may influence your decision. On the plus side, the male does not shed his coat as dramatically as the female. Generally, he will blow his coat just once a year, rather than the female's twice yearly cycle.

If you opt for a female, you will need to cope with her seasons, which will start at around seven to eight months of age and occur approximately every nine months thereafter. During the three-week period of a season, you will need to keep your bitch away from entire males (males that have not been neutered) to eliminate the risk of an unwanted pregnancy.

Many pet owners opt for neutering, which puts an end to the seasons, and also and has attendant health benefits. The operation, known as spaying, is usually carried out at some point after the first season. The best plan is to seek advice from your vet.

An entire male may not cause many problems, although some do have a stronger tendency to mark, which could include in the house. However, training will usually put a stop to this. An entire male will also be on the lookout for bitches in season, and this may lead to difficulties, depending on your circumstances.

Neutering (castrating) a male is a relatively simple operation, and there are associated health benefits. Again, you should seek advice from your vet.

Color

The Alaskan Malamute comes in a wonderful array of colors – grey, black, sable, red and white – and the shadings can be very subtle, varying from dog to dog. Mals have white markings on the body, and there are also a variety of facial markings – cap, mask, blaze, star, goggles, eye shadow, open face, closed face – which are all highly distinctive.

In this breed, there are no rare colors or markings; they all have equal merit, so it all comes down to personal preference.

More than one?

Alaskan Malamutes are not the most sociable breed and you need to take great care if you introduce a second dog to your household. Malamutes can be aggressive, so if you decide to increase your numbers, proceed with extreme caution.

Most important of all, do not choose two Mals of the same sex. Two females together, or two males together, will not get on. The best plan is to get opposite sexes, and, unless you are going to get involved in breeding, you should get one, or both, neutered.

If you plan to keep a mixed pair of Malamutes, do not make the mistake of taking on two puppies at the same time. Looking after one puppy is hard work, but taking on two pups at the same time is more than double the workload. House training is a nightmare as, often, you don't even know which puppy is making mistakes, and training is impossible unless you separate the two puppies and give them one-on-one attention. With a strong-willed Malamute, it is essential to establish a positive relationship, based on trust and respect; this is highly unlikely to happen if you are trying to cope with two boisterous youngsters.

It is a win-win scenario for the puppies; they will never be bored as they have each other to play with. However, the likelihood is that they will form a close bond with each other, and you will come a poor second.

If you do decide to add to your Malamute population, wait at least 18 months so your first dog is fully trained and settled before taking on a puppy.

An older dog

You may decide to miss out on the puppy phase and take on an older dog instead. Such a dog may be harder to track down, but sometimes a breeder may have a youngster that is not suitable for showing, but is perfect for a family pet. Malamutes with woolly coats come under this category; they are high maintenance in terms of grooming, but you may feel this is something you are prepared to take on. For more information, see page 110.

Taking on two Mals of a similar age is a recipe for disaster.

In some cases, a breeder may rehome a female when her breeding career is at an end so she will enjoy the benefits of getting more individual attention.

There are advantages to taking on an older dog, as you know exactly what you are getting. But the upheaval of changing homes can be quite upsetting, so you will need to have plenty of patience during the settling in period.

Rehoming a rescued dog

We are fortunate that the number of Alaskan Malamutes that end up in rescue is still relatively small, but it is inevitable that it will increase as the breed becomes more popular.

In many cases, a Mal ends up in rescue through no fault of his own. The reasons are various, ranging from illness or death of the original owner to family breakdown, changing jobs, or even the arrival of a new baby. However, there are Malamutes that are put up for rescue because their owners cannot cope with them, and they may well have some training and behavioral issues.

It is unlikely that you will find a Malamute in an all-breed rescue centre, but the specialist breed clubs run rescue schemes, and this will be your best option if you decide to go down this route.

Try to find out as much as you can about a dog's history so you know exactly what you are taking on. You need to be realistic about what you are capable of achieving so you can be sure you can give the dog in question a permanent home.

Again, you need to give a rescued Malamute plenty of time and patience as he settles into his new home, but if all goes well, you will have the reward of knowing that you have given your dog a second chance.

Sourcing a puppy

Your aim is to find a healthy puppy that is typical of the breed, and has been reared with the greatest possible care. Where do you start?

A tried-and-trusted method of finding a puppy is to attend a dog show where your chosen breed is being exhibited. This will give you the opportunity to see lots of different Alaskan Malamutes, and to see the range of colors available. When you look closely, you will also see there are different 'types' on show. They are all pure-bred Malamutes, but breeders produce dogs with a family likeness, so you can see which type you prefer.

When judging has been completed, talk to the exhibitors and find out more about their dogs. They may not have puppies available, but most will be planning a litter, and you may decide to put your name on a waiting list.

Internet research

The Internet is an excellent resource, but when it comes to finding a puppy, use it with care:

DO go to the website of your national kennel club.

Both the American Kennel Club (AKC) and the

Kennel Club (KC) have excellent websites, which will give you information about the Alaskan Malamute as a breed, and what to look for when choosing a puppy. You will also find contact details for specialist breed clubs (see below).

Both sites have lists of puppies available, and you can look out for breeders of merit (AKC) and assured breeders (KC) which indicates that a code of conduct has been adhered to.

DO find details of specialist breed clubs.

On breed club websites you will find lots of useful information that will help you to care for your Malamute. There may be contact details of breeders in your area, or you may need to go through the club secretary. Some websites also have a list of breeders that have puppies available. The advantage of going through a breed club is that members will follow a code of ethics, and this will give you some guarantees regarding breeding stock and health checks.

DO NOT look at puppies for sale.

There are legitimate Malamute breeders with their own websites, and they may, occasionally, advertise a litter, although in most cases reputable breeders have waiting lists for their puppies. The danger comes from unscrupulous breeders that produce puppies purely for profit, with no thought for the health of the dogs they breed from and no care given to rearing the litter. Photos of puppies are hard to resist, but never make a decision based purely on an advertisement. You need to find out who the breeder is, and have the opportunity to visit their premises and inspect the litter before making a decision.

Questions, questions, questions

When you find a breeder with puppies available, you will have lots of questions to ask. These should include the following:

- Where have the puppies been reared? Hopefully, they will be in a home environment, which gives them the best possible start in life.

- How many are in the litter?

- What is the split of males and females?

- What colors are available?

- How many have already been spoken for? The breeder will probably be keeping a puppy to show or for breeding, and there may be others on a waiting list.

- Can I see the mother with her puppies?

- What age are the puppies?

Facing page: Find out as much as you can about the health status of the puppies' parents and their close relatives.

- When will they be ready to go to their new homes?

Bear in mind puppies need to be with their mother and siblings until they are eight weeks of age, otherwise they miss out on vital learning and communication skills which will have a detrimental effect on them for the rest of their lives.

You should also be prepared to answer a number of searching questions so the breeder can check if you are suitable as a potential owner of one of their precious puppies.

You will be asked some or all of the following questions:

- What is your home set up?

- Do you have children/grandchildren?

- What are their ages?

- Is there somebody at home the majority of the time?

- What is your previous experience with dogs?

- Do you have plans to show or work your Malamute?

The breeder is not being intrusive; they need to understand the type of home you will be able to provide in order to make the right match. Do not be offended by this; the breeder is doing it for both the dog's benefit and also for yours.

Be very wary of a breeder who does not ask you questions. He or she may be more interested in making money out of the puppies rather than ensuring that they go to good homes. They may also have taken other short cuts which may prove disastrous, and very expensive, in terms of vet bills or plain heartache.

Health issues

In common with all pure-bred dogs, the Alaskan Malamute suffers from some hereditary problems so you need to talk to the breeder about the health status of breeding stock and find out if there are any issues of concern. There are health clearances for hip dysplasia and some eye disorders, which should have been carried out, with the relevant paperwork available to view.

For information on inherited conditions, see page 180.

Puppy watching

Alaskan Malamute puppies are totally irresistible; they look like wooly teddy bears, and when you see a litter you will want to take the whole lot home with you!

However, you must try to put your feelings to one side so that you can make an informed choice. You need to be 100 per cent confident that the breeding stock is healthy, and the puppies have been reared with love and care, before making a commitment to buy.

Viewing a litter

It is a good idea to have a mental checklist of what to look out for when you visit a breeder. You want to see:

- A clean, hygienic environment.

- Puppies who are out-going and friendly, and eager to meet you.

- A sweet-natured mother who is ready to show off her pups.

- Puppies that are well covered, but not pot-bellied, which could be an indication of worms.

- Bright eyes, with no sign of soreness or discharge.

- Clean ears that smell fresh.

- No discharge from the nose.

- Clean rear ends – matting could indicate upset tummies.

- Lively pups who are keen to play.

It is important that you see the mother with her puppies as this will give you a good idea of the temperament they are likely to inherit. It is also helpful if you can see other close relatives so you can see the type of Malamute the breeder produces.

In most cases, you will not be able to see the father (sire) as most breeders will travel some distance to find a stud dog that is not too close to their own bloodlines and complements their bitch. However, you should be able to see photos of him and be given the chance to examine his pedigree and show record.

Companion puppy

If you are looking for a Malamute as a companion, you should be guided by the breeder who will have spent hours and hours puppy watching, and will know each of the pups as individuals. It is tempting to choose a puppy yourself, but the breeder will take into account your family set up and lifestyle and will help you to pick the most suitable puppy.

The breeder will have got to know each of the puppies as individuals.

Sports puppy

If you are looking for a puppy to work, the best plan is to research the pedigrees and find out whether dogs from the breeding lines in question have been successful in canine sports. It may not be the sport you are planning to get involved with – for example, you may be planning an agility career for your Mal rather than sled racing – but it will prove that there are talented dogs in the bloodlines.

When choosing a puppy, look for a lively individual who is interested in everything that is going on. In addition, you want a puppy that is eager to play and who is responsive to your body language and your voice.

Show puppy

If you are buying a puppy with the hope of showing him, make sure you make this clear to the breeder. A lot of planning goes into producing a litter, and although all the puppies will have been reared with equal care, there will be one or two that have show potential.

Ideally, recruit a breed expert to inspect the puppies with you, so you have the benefit of their objective evaluation. The breeder will also be there to help as they will want to ensure that only the best of their stock is exhibited in the show ring.

It is important to bear in mind that puppies go through many phases as they are developing. A promising puppy may well go through an ugly duckling phase, and all you can do is hope that he blossoms! However, if your Malamute fails to make the grade in the show ring, he will still be an outstanding companion and a much-loved member of your family.

It takes a breed specialist to evaluate show potential.

A Malamute-
friendly home

It may seem an age before your Malamute puppy is ready to leave the breeder and move to his new home. But you can fill the time by getting your home ready, and buying the equipment you will need. These preparations apply to a new puppy but, in reality, they are the means of creating an environment that is safe and secure for your Mal throughout his life.

In the home

Nothing is safe when a puppy is about – especially an Alaskan Malamute. The Mal will investigate everything he comes across, and even as a puppy he is a highly destructive chewer. Not only does this mean that your prized possessions are under threat; it could also have disastrous consequences for your puppy.

The best plan is to decide which rooms your Mal will have access to, and make these areas puppy friendly.

Trailing electric cables are a major hazard and these will need to be secured out of reach. You will need to make sure all cupboards and storage units cannot be opened – or broken into. This applies particularly in the kitchen, where you may store cleaning materials, and other substances which could be toxic to dogs. There are a number of household plants that are poisonous, so these will need to relocated, along with breakable ornaments.

While your Malamute is growing, his joints are vulnerable so you need to reduce the risk of injury. Most owners find it is easier to make upstairs off-limits right from the start. The best way of doing this is to use a baby gate, and these can also be useful if you want to limit your Mal's freedom in any other part of the house.

In the garden

Secure fencing is essential for this large, powerful breed. Not all Alaskan Malamutes are escape artists, but there are some who prove to be very determined so you need to ensure your garden is secure. Fencing should be a minimum of 1.6m (5 ft), and gates must have secure fastenings.

Even so, you should not allow your Malamute to spend lengthy periods in the garden when he is not supervised. A bored Malamute is far more likely to escape. His other options are to occupy himself by howling or digging up your prized flower-beds.

If you are a keen gardener, the best plan is to protect your plants from unwanted attention by fencing them off so you have a 'people' garden and a 'dog' garden. Malamutes are great diggers – possibly a throwback to the days when they had to dig dens in the snow – but this is not helpful in a garden! You may find that your Mal becomes more civilized as he matures, but there are some that have a lifelong passion for digging.

You will also need to designate a toileting area. This will assist the house-training process, and it will also make cleaning up easier. For information on house-training, see page 92.

House rules

Before your puppy comes home, hold a family conference to decide on the house rules. You need to decide which rooms your puppy will have access to, and establish whether he is to be allowed on the furniture or not. Remember, with a Mal, it is important to start as you mean to go on. You cannot invite a puppy on to the sofa for cuddles only to decide in a few months' time that this is no longer desirable. A Mal is a pushy dog and needs to know where his boundaries lie. If house rules are applied consistently, he will understand what is – and what is not – allowed, and he will learn to respect you and co-operate with you.

Buying equipment

There are some essential items of equipment you will need for your Alaskan Malamute. If you choose wisely, much of it will last for many years to come.

Indoor crate

Rearing a puppy is so much easier if you invest in an indoor crate. It provides a safe haven for your puppy at night, when you have to go out during the days and at other times when you cannot supervise him. A puppy needs a base where he feels safe and secure, and where he can rest undisturbed. An indoor crate

Facing page: Buy good-quality equipment which will stand the test of time – and Malamute teeth!

provides the perfect den, and many adults continue to use them throughout their lives.

Obviously you need to buy a crate that will be large enough to accommodate your Mal when he is fully grown. He needs space to stand up, turn around, and lie at full stretch.

You will also need to consider where you are going to locate the crate. The kitchen is usually the most suitable place as this is the hub of family life. Try to find a snug corner where the puppy can rest when he wants to, but where he can also see what is going on around him, and still be with the family.

Beds and bedding

The crate will need to be lined with bedding and the best type to buy is synthetic fleece. This is warm and cosy, and, as moisture soaks through it, your puppy will not have a wet bed when he is tiny and is still unable to go through the night without relieving himself. This type of bedding is machine washable and easy to dry. Buy two pieces, so you have one to use while the other is in the wash.

If you have purchased a crate, you may not feel the need to buy an extra bed, although many Malamutes like to have a bed in the family room so they feel part of household activities. There is an amazing array of dog-beds to chose from – duvets, bean bags, cushions, baskets, igloos, mini-four posters – so you can take your pick! However, you do need to bear in mind that a Mal can be very destructive, so you would be advised to delay making a major investment until your puppy has gone through the worst of the chewing phase.

It is also worth remembering that a Malamute has a very thick coat, so he has no need to seek out additional warmth.

Collar and leash

You may think that it is not worth buying a collar for the first few weeks, but the sooner your pup gets used to it, the better. All you need is a lightweight collar to start with; you will need something more substantial as your Mal becomes bigger and stronger.

A nylon leash is suitable for early leash training, as long as the fastening is secure. You will probably need a leather leash, with a trigger fastening, when your Mal is full grown, as nylon leashes tend to chafe your hands.

Harness

Many Mal owners prefer to use a harness rather than a collar and leash. This is a matter of personal preference, but it does seem to give good control, and can prevent a tendency to pull.

There are many different types of harness; the golden rule is to make sure the harness you buy is well padded, and is fitted by an expert so that your Mal can move freely with no trace of discomfort.

ID

Your Alaskan Malamute needs to wear some form of ID when he is out in public places. This can be in the form of a disc, engraved with your contact details, attached to the collar. When your Mal is full-grown, you can buy a collar embroidered with your contact details, which eliminates the danger of the disc becoming detached from the collar.

You may also wish to consider a permanent form of ID. Increasingly breeders are getting puppies' micro-chipped before they go to their new homes. A micro-chip is the size of a grain of rice and is 'injected' under the skin, usually between the shoulder blades, with a special needle. The chip has tiny barbs on it, which dig into the tissue around where it lies, so it does not migrate from that spot.

Each chip has its own unique identification number which can only be read by a special scanner. That ID number is then registered on a national database with your name and details, so that if ever your dog is lost, he can be taken to any vet or rescue center where he is scanned and then you are contacted.

If your puppy has not been micro-chipped, you can ask your vet to do it.

Bowls

Your Mal will need two bowls; one for food, and one for fresh drinking water, which should always be readily available. A stainless steel bowl is a good choice for a food bowl as it is tough and hygienic. Plastic bowls may be chewed, and there is a danger that bacteria can collect in the small cracks that may appear.

You can opt for a second stainless steel bowl for drinking water, or you may prefer a heavier ceramic bowl that will not be knocked over so easily.

Food

The breeder will let you know what your puppy is eating and should provide a full diet sheet to guide you through the first six months of your puppy's feeding regime – how much they are eating per meal, how many meals per day, when to increase the amounts given per meal and when to reduce the meals per day.

The breeder may provide you with some food when you go and collect your puppy, but it is worth making enquiries in advance about the availability of the brand that is recommended.

Grooming equipment

When your puppy first arrives, he does not require extensive coat care, but he needs to get used to being groomed. You will need the following:

- A good-quality pin brush
- A slicker brush
- A combination metal comb with wide and narrow teeth

Facing page: Grooming is going to be a big part of your Mal's life.

- A grooming rake, to use when the coat is shedding

- Guillotine nail clippers

- Toothbrush (a finger brush is easiest to use) and specially-manufactured dog toothpaste.

- Cotton (cotton-wool) pads for cleaning the eyes and ears

Toys

Your guiding principle when choosing a toy for a Malamute is whether it is suitably robust to withstand chewing. Soft toys and plastic toys with squeakers should be avoided; opt for hard rubber toys, kongs (which can be filled with food), and tough tug toys.

You should also get into the habit of checking toys on a regular basis for signs of wear and tear. If your puppy swallows a chunk of rubber or plastic, it could cause an internal blockage. This could involve costly surgery to remove the offending item, or at worst it could prove fatal.

Finding a vet

Before your puppy arrives home, you should register with a vet. Visit some of the vets in your local area, and speak to other pet owners that you know, to see who they recommend. It is so important to find a good vet, almost as much as finding a good doctor for yourself. You need to find someone with whom you can build up a good rapport and have complete faith in. Word of mouth is really the best recommendation.

When you contact a veterinary practice, find out the following:

- Does the surgery run an appointment system?

- What are the arrangements for emergency, out-of-hours cover?

- Do any of the vets in the practice have experience treating Malamutes, or other Nordic breeds?

- What facilities are available at the practice?

If you are satisfied with what your find, and the staff appear to be helpful and friendly, book an appointment so your puppy can have a health check a couple of days after you collect him.

Settling in

When you first arrive home with your puppy, be careful not to overwhelm him. You and your family are hugely excited, but the puppy is in a completely strange environment with new sounds, smells and sights, which is a daunting experience, even for the boldest of pups.

Some puppies are very confident, wanting to play straightaway and quickly making friends; others need a little longer. Keep a close check on your Malamute's body language and reactions so you can proceed at a pace he is comfortable with.

First, let him explore the garden. He will probably need to relieve himself after the journey home, so take him to the allocated toileting area and when he performs give him plenty of praise.

When you take your puppy indoors, let him investigate again. Show him his crate, and encourage him to go in by throwing in a treat. Let him have a sniff, and allow him to go in and out as he

wishes. Later on, when he is tired, you can put him in the crate while you stay in the room. In this way he will learn to settle and will not think he is being abandoned.

It is a good idea to feed your puppy in his crate, at least to begin with, as this helps to build up a positive association. It will not be long before your Mal sees his crate as his own special den and will go there as a matter of choice. Some owners place a blanket over the crate, covering the back and sides, so that it is even more cosy and den-like.

Meeting the family

Resist the temptation to invite friends and neighbors to come and meet the new arrival; your puppy needs to focus on getting to know his new family for the first few days. Try not to swamp your Mal with too much attention; give him a chance to explore and find his feet. There will be plenty of time for cuddles later on!

If you have children in the family, you need to keep everything as calm as possible. Your puppy may not have met children before, and even if he has, he will still find them strange and unpredictable. A puppy can become alarmed by too much noise, or he may go to the opposite extreme and become over-excited, which can lead to mouthing and nipping.

The best plan is to get the children to sit on the floor and give each of them a treat. Each child can then call the puppy, stroke him, and offer a treat. In this way the puppy is making the decisions rather than being forced into interactions he may find stressful.

If he tries to nip or mouth, make sure there is a toy at the ready, so his attention can be diverted to something he is allowed to bite. If you do this consistently, he will learn to inhibit his desire to mouth when he is interacting with people.

Right from the start, impose a rule that the children are not allowed to pick up or carry the puppy. They can cuddle him when they are sitting on the floor. This may sound a little severe, but a wriggly puppy can be dropped in an instant, sometimes with disastrous consequences. If possible, try to make sure your Mal is only given attention when he has all four feet on the ground. This is a breed than can be boisterous so, if your pup learns that jumping up is not rewarding, it will pay dividends later on.

Involve all family members with the day-to-day care of your puppy; this will enable the bond to develop with the whole family as opposed to just one person. Encourage the children to train and reward the puppy, teaching him to follow their commands without question.

The animal family

Great care must be taken when introducing a puppy to a resident dog to ensure that relations get off on the right footing. As highlighted earlier, same sex pairs should be avoided, but even with a mixed pair you need to be vigilant and supervise early interactions.

Your adult dog may be allowed to meet the puppy at the breeder's home, which is ideal as the older dog will not feel threatened if he is away from home. But if this is not possible, allow your dog to smell the puppy's bedding (the bedding supplied by the breeder is fine) before they actually meet so he familiarizes himself with the puppy's scent.

The garden is the best place for introducing the puppy, as the adult will regard it as neutral territory. He will probably take a great interest in the puppy and sniff him all over. Most puppies are naturally submissive in this situation, and your pup may lick the other dog's mouth or roll over on to his back. Try not to interfere, as this is the natural way that dogs get to know each other.

You will only need to intervene if the older dog is too boisterous, and alarms the puppy. In this case, it is a good idea to put the adult on his lead so you have some measure of control.

It rarely takes long for an adult to accept a puppy, as he does not constitute a threat. This will be underlined if you make a big fuss of the older dog so that he has no reason to feel jealous. But no matter how well the two dogs are getting on, do not leave them alone unless one is crated.

Feline friends

An Alaskan Malamute will learn to co-exist with a cat, as long as he is trained from puppyhood to understand cats are not for chasing. You will need to work very hard at early interactions and progress step by step, making sure the pair are never left alone together.

It may be easier if the cat is confined in a carrier for the first couple of meetings so your puppy has a chance to make his acquaintance in a controlled situation. Keep calling your puppy to you and rewarding him so that he does not focus too intently on the cat. You can then graduate to holding your puppy while the cat is free, again rewarding him with a treat every time he responds to you and looks away from the cat. When you allow your puppy to go free, make sure the cat has an easy escape route, just in case he tries to chase.

This is an ongoing process, but all the time your Mal is learning that he is rewarded for ignoring the cat. In time, the novelty will wear off and the pair will live in harmony.

Feeding

The breeder will generally provide enough food for the first few days so the puppy does not have to cope with a change in diet – and possible digestive upset – along with all the stress of moving home.

Some puppies eat up their food from the first meal onwards, others are more concerned by their new surroundings and are too distracted to eat. Do not worry unduly if your puppy seems disinterested in his food for the first day or so. Give him 10 minutes to eat what he wants and then remove the leftovers and start afresh at the next meal. Obviously if you have any concerns about your puppy in the first few days, seek advice from your vet.

The Alaskan Malamute can be possessive over his food, and this is an issue that should be tackled from day one. If you have children, you need to establish a rule that no one is to go near the dog when he is feeding. This is sound commonsense, and removes all risk of problems arising, no matter how unintentional they may be.

However, there is plenty of scope for you to work on your Mal's manners so that he does not feel protective of his food bowl. You can do this by giving him half his ration, and then dropping food around his bowl. This will stop him guarding his bowl and, at the same time, he will see your presence in a positive light. You can also call him away from the bowl and reward him with some food – maybe something extra special – which he can take from your hand.

Start doing this as soon as your puppy arrives in his new home, and continue working on it throughout his life. Remember, food is a top priority for your Mal; he will respect you as the provider and, if you interact with him as described, he will trust you and will not feel threatened.

The first night

Your puppy will have spent the first weeks of his life with his mother or curled up with his siblings. He is then taken from everything he knows as familiar, lavished with attention by his new family – and then comes bed time when he is left all alone. It is little wonder that he feels abandoned.

The best plan is to establish a night-time routine, and then stick to it so that your puppy knows what is expected of him. Take your puppy out into the garden to relieve himself, and then settle him in his crate. Some people leave a low light on for the puppy at night for the first week, others have tried a radio as company or a ticking clock. A covered hot-water bottle, filled with warm water, can also be a comfort. Like people, puppies are all individuals and what works for one, does not necessarily work for another, so it is a matter of trial and error.

Be very positive when you leave your puppy on his own. Do not linger, or keep returning, which will only make the situation more difficult. It is inevitable that he will protest to begin with, but if you stick to your routine, he will accept that he gets left at night – and you always return in the morning.

Rescued dogs

Settling an older, rescued dog in the home is very similar to a puppy in as much as you will need to make the same preparations regarding his homecoming. As with a puppy, an older dog will need you to be consistent, so start as you mean to go on.

There is often an initial honeymoon period when you first bring a rescued dog home. He will be on his best behaviour for the first few weeks, then the true nature of the dog will gradually emerge, so be prepared for subtle changes in his behavior. It may be advisable to register with a reputable training club, so you can seek advice on any training or behavioral issues at an early stage.

Above all, remember that a rescued dog ceases to be a rescued dog the moment he enters his forever home and should be treated like any other family dog.

House
training

The Alaskan Malamute has a reputation for being difficult to house-train, but if you approach the task with a positive attitude, and you are prepared to put in the time and effort it requires – for as long as it takes – you will not encounter major problems.

The key to successful house-training is vigilance and consistency. If you establish a routine, and you stick to it, your puppy will understand what is required. Equally, you must be there to supervise him at all times – except when he is safely tucked up in his crate. It is when a puppy is left to wander from room to room that accidents are most likely to happen.

As discussed earlier, you will have allocated a toileting area in your garden when preparing for your puppy's homecoming. You need to take your puppy to this area every time he needs to relieve himself so he builds up an association and knows why you have brought him out to the garden.

Establish a routine and make sure you take your puppy out at the following times:

- First thing in the morning

- After mealtimes

- On waking from a sleep

- Following a play session

- Last thing at night.

A puppy should be taken out to relieve himself every two hours as an absolute minimum. If you can manage an hourly trip out, so much the better. The more often your puppy gets it 'right', the quicker he will learn to be clean in the house. It helps if you use a verbal cue, such as "busy", when your pup is performing and, in time, this will trigger the desired response.

Do not be tempted to put your puppy out on the doorstep in the hope that he will toilet on his own. Most pups simply sit there, waiting to get back inside the house! No matter how bad the weather is, accompany your puppy and give him lots of praise when he performs correctly.

Do not rush back inside as soon as he has finished, or your puppy might start to delay in the hope of prolonging his time outside with you. Praise him, have a quick game – and then you can both return indoors.

When accidents happen

No matter how vigilant you are, there are bound to be accidents. If you witness the accident, take your puppy outside immediately, and give him lots of praise if he finishes his business out there.

If you are not there when he has an accident, do not scold him when you discover what has happened. He will not remember what he has done and will not understand why you are cross with him. Simply clean it up and resolve to be more vigilant next time.

Make sure you use a deodorizer, available in pet stores, when you clean up, otherwise your pup will be drawn to the smell and may be tempted to use the same spot again.

Facing page:
Remember you are
usually to blame
for lapses in house
training....

Choosing a diet

There are so many different types of dog food on sale – all claiming to be the best – so how do you know what is likely to suit your Alaskan Malamute? This is a substantial dog that needs a well-balanced diet suited to his individual requirements.

When choosing a diet, there are basically three categories:

Complete

This is probably the most popular diet as it is easy to feed and is specially formulated with all the nutrients your dog needs. This means that you should not add any supplements, or you may upset the nutritional balance.

Most complete diets come in different life stages – puppy, adult maintenance and senior, so this means

that your Malamute is getting what he needs when he is growing, during adulthood, and as he becomes older. You can even get prescription diets for dogs with particular health issues.

Generally, an adult maintenance diet should contain 21-24 per cent protein and 10-14 per cent fat. Protein levels should be higher in puppy diets, and reduced in veteran diets. If you are working your Malamute on a regular basis, you may need a diet for active working dogs, which will contain more fat and protein.

There are many different brands to choose from so it is advisable to seek advice from your puppy's breeder, who will have lengthy experience of feeding Malamutes.

Canned/pouches

This type of food is usually fed with hard biscuit, and most Malamutes find it very appetizing. However, the ingredients – and the nutritional value – do vary significantly between the different brands so you will need to check the label. This type of food often has a high moisture content, so you need to be sure your Mal is getting all the nutrition he needs.

Homemade

There are some owners who like to prepare meals

especially for their dogs – and it is probably much appreciated. The danger is that although the food is tasty, and your Malamute may enjoy the variety, you cannot be sure that it has the correct nutritional balance.

If this is a route you want to go down, you will need to find out the exact ratio of fats, carbohydrates, proteins, minerals and vitamins that are needed, which is quite an undertaking.

The Barf (Biologically Appropriate Raw Food) diet is another, more natural approach to feeding. Dogs are fed a diet mimicking what they would have eaten in the wild, consisting of raw meat, bone, muscle, fat, and vegetable matter. Alaskan Malamutes thrive on this diet so it is certainly worth considering. There are now a number of companies that specialize in producing the Barf diet in frozen form, which will make your job a lot easier.

A regime of two meals a day will suit most adult Mals.

Feeding regime

When your puppy arrives in his new home he will need four meals, evenly spaced throughout the day. You may decide to keep to the diet recommended by your puppy's breeder, and if your pup is thriving there is no need to change. However, if your puppy is not doing well on the food, or you have problems with supply, you will need to make a change.

When switching diets, it is very important to do it on a gradual basis, changing over from one food to the next, a little at a time, and spreading the transition over a week to 10 days. This will avoid the risk of digestive upset.

When your puppy is around 12 weeks, you can cut out one of his meals; he may well have started to leave some of his food indicating he is ready to do this. By six months, he can move on to two meals a day – a regime that will suit him for the rest of his life.

Bones and chews

Puppies love to chew, and many adults also enjoy gnawing on a bone. Bones should always be hard and uncooked; rib bones and poultry bones must be avoided as they can splinter. Dental chews, and some of the manufactured rawhide chews, are safe, but they should only be given under supervision.

Ideal weight

In order to help to keep your Alaskan Malamute in good health it is necessary to monitor his weight. It is all too easy for the pounds to pile on, and this can result in serious health problems.

The major danger is feeding too much food in relation to the amount of energy your dog is expending. This is easily done if you follow feeding guidelines on packet foods, rather than monitoring your dog's individual weight and lifestyle.

It can be hard to assess a Malamute's weight because of his dense coat, but a good guide is to look at him from above, and make sure you can see a definite 'waist'. You should be able to feel his ribs, but not see them.

In order to keep a close check on your Malamute's weight, get into the habit of visiting your veterinary surgery on a monthly basis so that you can weigh him. You can keep a record of his weight so you can make adjustments if necessary.

If you are concerned that your Mal is putting on too much weight, consult your vet who will help you to plan a suitable diet.

Caring
for your
Malamute

The Alaskan Malamute was bred to live and work in the most extreme conditions so he had to be tough and easy to care for. Malamutes that are kept as pet dogs are relatively low maintenance, but like all animals, a Mal has his own special needs, which you must to take on board.

Puppy coat care

When your puppy arrives home, he will be an adorable ball of fluff; his coat will bear little relation to the adult coat that will develop.

For the most part, a Mal puppy does not need very much coat care, but do not make the mistake of waiting until he needs to be groomed. The inevitable outcome of this will be an almighty struggle and your Mal will build up a bad association with the whole process of being groomed.

Start by handling your puppy all over, stroking him from his head to his tail. Lift up each paw in turn, and reward him with a treat when he co-operates. Then roll him over on to his back and tickle his tummy; this is a very vulnerable position for a dog to adopt, so do not force the issue. Be firm but gentle, and give your Mal lots of praise when he does as you ask.

When your Mal is happy to be handled in this way, you can introduce a brush and start working through the coat. Initially, just spend a few minutes brushing the coat, and then reward him. In this way, he will gradually learn to accept the attention, and will relax while you groom him.

Adult grooming

The Alaskan Malamute has a thick weather-resistant topcoat composed of guard hairs, and a dense, oily undercoat, which is designed to give insulation in the harsh Arctic weather. One of the major advantages of the Malamute's coat – at least for his human family – is that it is almost completely free from odor. The coat does not tangle, but the Mal is a prodigious shedder, which means that thorough routine grooming is essential. This is also the best way of removing dirt and debris, as frequent bathing will destroy the natural oils in the coat.

Start by working through the coat with a slicker brush, starting from the neck and progressing along the body to the tail. The coat is longer on the chest, down the sides of the body, on the hind legs and tail, and so these areas will need more attention. Brush in the direction the coat lies.

When you have groomed through the coat with a slicker brush, use a pin brush, which will get right through to the undercoat.

The coat will then need to be combed through. This should be relatively easy if you have done a good job brushing the coat.

Some groomers use a technique known as 'line combing' where they part the coat and comb in small lines or sections, which can be particularly helpful when a Mal is shedding.

An Alaskan Malamute will generally shed his coat twice a year – in the Spring and in the autumn. This does not mean the rest of the year is free from moulting – far from it – but these are the times when a Mal will have a major shed, which is referred to as 'blowing' the coat. This major coat loss may be restricted to the undercoat, but sometimes a Mal will shed his topcoat as well. When this happens your Mal will look almost unrecognizable for a few weeks before the coat grows back and is restored to its former glory.

Males do not blow their coats as dramatically as females, and this may happen only once a year. Beware of a major 'blow' when your Mal is around 18 months of age as he sheds his puppy coat ready for the adult coat to come thorough.

Start by grooming the whole coat with a slicker brush.

Brush in the direction the coat lies.

Now comb through the coat.

Make sure you reach the undercoat.

The wooly coat

This refers to a coat that is longer, thicker and oilier that the correct Malamute coat. However, the major consideration is that this coat does not shed naturally and, if uncared for, the dead hair will form clumps and mats which will be a source of discomfort, and can also exacerbate skin problems, such as hot-spots (see page 186).

A Malamute with a wooly coat cannot be exhibited in the show ring as the topcoat in some areas may grow too long for the Breed Standard. Dogs with this incorrect coat should also be excluded from breeding programs. However, a Mal with this coat type will make a perfectly good pet, as long as the owner is prepared to take on the extra workload.

Wooly Mals need to be brushed and combed every day, paying particular attention to the undercoat, which will come out with gentle assistance. In some cases, clipping may be a sensible option if time is limited. Even though this changes the appearance of your Mal, it may be beneficial for him in the long run.

Show presentation

The Alaskan Malamute should be shown in his natural state, so coat care is a year-round endeavor rather than last minute preparation.

Some exhibitors bath their dog the day before a show, but care need to be taken to ensure the 'stiff' guard hairs do not become too soft in texture. There are specially formulated shampoos designed to protect this type of coat. Extensive grooming is required before the show, and often an exhibitor will brush the coat – firstly with the natural lay of the coat, and then in the opposite direction, to give a stand-off appearance.

There should be no trimming, except to neaten around the paws. Some exhibitors tidy up the facial hair, but this is matter of personal choice.

Routine care

In addition to grooming, you will need to carry out some other routine care.

Eyes

Check the eyes for signs of soreness or discharge. You can use a piece of cotton (cotton-wool) – a separate piece for each eye – and wipe away any debris.

Ears

The ears should be clean and free from odor. You can buy specially-manufactured ear wipes, or you can use a piece of cotton (cotton-wool) to clean them if necessary. Do not probe into the ear canal or you risk doing more harm than good.

Teeth

Dental disease is becoming more prevalent among dogs so teeth cleaning should be seen as an essential part of your care regime. The build up of tartar on the teeth can result in tooth decay, gum infection and bad breath, and if it is allowed to accumulate, you may have no option but to get the teeth cleaned under anesthetic.

When your Malamute is still a puppy, accustom him to teeth cleaning so it becomes a matter of routine. Dog toothpaste comes in a variety of meaty flavours, which your Mal will like, so you can start by putting some toothpaste on your finger and gently rubbing his teeth. You can then progress to using a finger brush or a toothbrush, whichever you find most convenient.

Remember to reward your Mal when he co-operates and then he will positively look forward to his teeth-cleaning sessions.

Nails

Nail trimming is a task dreaded by many owners – and many dogs – but, again, if you start early on, your Malamute will get used to the procedure.

If your dog has white nails, you will be able to see the quick (the vein that runs through the nail), which you must avoid at all costs. If you cut the quick it will bleed profusely and cause considerable discomfort. Obviously, the task is much harder in dark nails as you cannot see the quick. The best policy is to trim little and often so the nails don't grow too long, and you do not risk cutting too much and catching the quick.

If you are worried about trimming your Malamute's nails, go to your vet so you can see it done properly. If you are still concerned, you can always use the services of a professional groomer.

Exercise

The Alaskan Malamute is a large, powerful dog, built to pull heavy loads over long distances. As such, he has tremendous stamina and powers of endurance, and he needs an outlet for his energy.

This is where the problem lies for many Malamute owners. This is a dog with a strong prey drive, and he cannot be trusted off lead if there are opportunities to hunt.

Accustom your Mal to nail trimming from an early age.

Not only could he cause trouble with neighborhood cats, or any other livestock, he is a danger to himself. A Malamute that has picked up a scent will be deaf to your calls, and his instinct to chase may send him right into the path of an oncoming car.

If you have a Malamute, you need to keep him on an extending leash, or find an enclosed area where it is safe for him to run. The best option is to get involved in one of the canine sports, such as mushing, canicross or bikejoring, which will give your Mal the perfect opportunity to exercise, as well as giving him mental stimulation.

The older Malamute

We are fortunate the Malamute has a good life expectancy for a big dog – generally around 12 years – and you are unlikely to see any significant changes until he reaches double figures.

The older Malamute will sleep more, and he may be reluctant to go for longer walks. He may show signs of stiffness when he gets up from his bed, but these generally ease when he starts moving. Some older Malamutes may have impaired vision, and some may become a little deaf, but as long as their senses do not deteriorate dramatically, this is something older dogs learn to live with.

If you treat your older Mal with kindness and consideration, he will enjoy his later years and suffer the minimum of discomfort. It is advisable to switch him over to a senior diet, which is more suited to his needs, and you may need to adjust the quantity, as he will not be burning up the calories as he did when he was younger and more energetic. Make sure his sleeping quarters are warm and free from drafts, and if he gets wet, make sure you dry him thoroughly.

Most important of all, be guided by your Malamute. He will have good days when he feels up to going for a walk, and other days when he would prefer to potter in the garden. If you have a younger dog at home, this may well stimulate your Mal to take more of an interest in what is going on, but make sure he is not pestered as he needs to rest undisturbed when he is tired.

Letting go

Inevitably there comes a time when your Malamute is not enjoying a good quality of life, and you need to make the painful decision to let him go. We would all wish that our dogs died, painlessly, in their sleep but, unfortunately, this is rarely the case.

However, we can allow our dogs to die with dignity, and to suffer as a little as possible, and this should be our way of saying thank you for the wonderful companionship they have given us.

When you feel the time is drawing close, talk to your vet, who will be able to make an objective assessment of your Malamute's condition and will help you to make the right decision.

This is the hardest thing you will ever have to do as a dog owner, and it is only natural to grieve for your beloved Mal. But eventually, you will be able to look back on the happy memories of times spent together, and this will bring much comfort. You may, in time, feel that your life is not complete without a Malamute, and you will feel ready to welcome a new puppy into your home.

Social skills

To live in the modern world, without fears and anxieties, an Alaskan Malamute needs to receive an education in social skills so that he learns to cope calmly and confidently in a wide variety of situations.

This is true of all breeds, but for a big, powerful dog it is of paramount importance. A Malamute is naturally an independent thinker, and he can be assertive when he is in the company of other dogs. He needs to learn acceptable behavior right from the start.

Early learning

The breeder will have begun a program of socialization by getting the puppies used to all the sights and sounds of a busy household. You need to continue this when your pup arrives in his new home, making sure he is not worried by household equipment, such the vacuum cleaner or the washing machine, and that he gets used to unexpected noises from the radio and television.

As already highlighted, it is important that you handle your puppy on a regular basis so he will accept grooming and other routine care, and will not be worried if he has to be examined by the vet.

To begin with, your puppy needs to get used to all the members of his new family, but then you should give him the opportunity to meet friends and other visitors to the house. The Mal is naturally friendly and outgoing but, because of his size, he needs to learn appropriate greeting behavior. This should start right from the beginning; your puppy may not be big enough to cause trouble, but if he gets into the habit of jumping up at people, it is potentially dangerous, and will become increasingly hard to correct.

When visitors arrive at your home, adopt the following procedure:

- Make sure your Mal is on the leash so you are in control.

- When you go to answer the door, make sure you have treats at the ready.

- Ask your Mal to "Sit" before opening the door, and reward him with a treat.

- When you open the door, make sure your Mal remains in the Sit, correcting him (and rewarding again) if necessary.

- The next step is to ask the visitor to give your Mal a treat, but makes sure he remains in the Sit.

This process is quite long-winded so the best plan is to practice with friends who are used to dogs so your Mal understands what is required.

If you do not have children of your own, make sure your puppy has the chance to meet and play with other people's children so he learns that humans come in small sizes, too.

The Alaskan Malamute is a large, powerful dog so he needs to learn appropriate greeting behavior.

The outside world

When your puppy has completed his vaccinations, he is ready to venture into the outside world. In most cases a Malamute puppy will take a lively interest in anything new and will relish the opportunity to broaden his horizons. However, there is a lot for a youngster to take on board, so do not swamp him with too many new experiences when you first set out.

The best plan is to start in a quiet area with light traffic, and only progress to a busier place when your puppy is ready. There is so much to see and hear – people (maybe carrying bags or umbrellas), pushchairs, bicycles, cars, trucks, buses, machinery – so give your puppy a chance to take it all in.

If he does appear worried, do not fall into the trap of sympathizing with him, or worse still, picking him up. This will only teach your pup that he had a good reason to be worried and, with luck, you will 'rescue' him if he feels scared.

Instead, give a little space so he does not have to confront whatever he is frightened of, and distract him with a few treats. Then encourage him to walk past, using a calm, no-nonsense approach. Your pup will take the lead from you, and will realize there is nothing to fear.

Your pup also needs to continue his education in

Facing page: Learn to read your Mal's body language so you understand his intentions.

canine manners, started by his mother and by his littermates, as he must be able to greet all dogs calmly, giving the signals that say he is friendly and offers no threat. If you have a friend who has a dog of sound temperament, this is an ideal beginning. As your puppy gets older and more established, you can widen his circle of canine acquaintances.

Training classes

A training class will give your Malamute the opportunity to work alongside other dogs in a controlled situation, and he will also learn to focus on you in a different, distracting environment. Both these lessons will be vital as your Malamute matures and becomes more assertive.

However, the training class needs to be of the highest caliber or you risk doing more harm than good. Before you go along with your puppy, attend a class as an observer to make sure you are happy with what goes on.

Find out the following:

- How much training experience do the instructors have?

- Are the classes divided into appropriate age categories?

- Do the instructors have experience training large dogs? They may not have worked with Malamutes, but do they have knowledge of the Nordic breeds?

- Do they use positive, reward-based training methods?

If the training class is well run, it is certainly worth attending. Both you and your Mal will learn useful training exercises; it will increase his social skills, and you will have the chance to talk to lots of like-minded dog enthusiasts.

A well-run training class will teach your Mal to focus on you despite the distractions of other dogs.

Training guidelines

We are fortunate that the Alaskan Malamute is an intelligent dog and he likes to please his human family. However, this is a dog with a strong, independent mind, and you need to earn his respect so that he is willing to co-operate with you.

You will be keen to get started, but in your rush to get training underway, do not neglect the fundamentals, which could make the difference between success and failure.

When you start training, try to observe the following guidelines:

- Choose an area that is free from distractions so your puppy will focus on you. You can progress to a more challenging environment as your pup progresses.

- Do not train your puppy just after he has eaten or when you have returned from exercise. He will either be too full, or too tired, to concentrate.

- Do not train if you are in a bad mood, or if you are short of time – these sessions always end in disaster!

- Make sure you have a reward your Malamute values – tasty treats, such as cheese or cooked liver, or an extra special toy.

- If you are using treats, make sure they are bite-size, otherwise you will lose momentum when your pup stops to chew on his treat.

- Keep your verbal cues simple, and always use the same one for each exercise. For example, when you ask your puppy to go into the Down position, the cue is "Down", not "Lie Down", "Get Down", or anything else... Remember your Mal does not speak English; he associates the sound of the word with the action.

- If your Malamute is finding an exercise difficult, break it down into small steps so it is easier to understand.

- Do not make your training sessions boring and repetitious. Your Mal will quickly lose interest – and this may diminish his respect for you.

Clicker training – clicking your Mal for the correct behavior and then rewarding – is a very effective method of training.

- Do not train for too long. Young puppies have a very short attention span.

- Always end training sessions on a positive note.

- Above all, have fun so you and your Mal both enjoy spending quality time together.

First lessons

Like all puppies, a young Alaskan Malamute will soak up new experiences like a sponge, so training should start from the time your pup arrives in his new home. It is so much easier to teach good habits rather than trying to correct your puppy when he has established an undesirable pattern of behavior.

Wearing a collar

You may, or may not, want your Malamute to wear a collar all the time; this may well depend if he is kenneled or not. But when he goes out in public places he will need to be on a leash, and so he should be used to the feel of a collar around his neck. The best plan is to accustom your pup to wearing a soft collar for a few minutes at a time until he gets used to it.

Fit the collar so that you can get at least two fingers between the collar and his neck. Then have a game to distract his attention. This will work for a few moments; then he will stop, put his back leg up behind his neck and scratch away at the peculiar itchy thing round his neck, which feels so odd.

Bend down, rotate the collar, pat him on the head and distract him by playing with a toy or giving him a treat. Once he has worn the collar for a few minutes each day, he will soon ignore it and become used to it.

Remember, never leave the collar on the puppy unsupervised, especially when he is outside in the garden or when he is in his crate, as it is could get snagged, causing serious injury.

Walking on the lead

Bear in mind that an Alaskan Malamute is bred to pull, so walking on a loose leash will not come naturally to him. A mature Mal is tremendously strong, and so you need to establish leash walking manners before he has a chance to get the upper hand.

Once your puppy is used to the collar, take him outside into your secure garden where there are no distractions.

Attach the leash and, to begin with, allow him to wander with the leash trailing, making sure it does not become snagged. Then pick up the leash and follow the pup where he wants to go; he needs to get used to the sensation of being attached to you.

The next stage is to get your Mal to follow you, and for this you will need some tasty treats. You can show him a treat in your hand, and then encourage him to follow you. Walk a few paces, and if he is co-operating, stop and reward him. If he puts on the brakes, simply change direction and lure him with the treat.

Next, introduce some changes of direction so your puppy is walking confidently alongside you. At this stage, introduce a verbal cue "Heel" when your puppy is in the correct position. You can then graduate to walking your puppy outside the home – as long as he has completed his vaccination program – starting in quiet areas and building up to busier environments.

Do not expect too much of your puppy too soon when you are leash walking away from home. He will be distracted by all the new sights and sounds he encounters, so concentrating on leash training will be difficult for him. Give him a chance to look and see, and reward him frequently when he is walking forward confidently on a loose leash.

Be prepared to spend a considerable amount of time establishing good leash-walking, as it will have far-reaching effects. A Malamute that pulls on the leash is a nightmare to live with, and you will soon start

The aim is for your Malamute to walk on a loose leash.

excluding him from expeditions where you know he will be a problem. However, if your Mal is trained to walk calmly beside you, on a loose leash, he will become your constant companion, and will be a pleasure to own.

Come when called

Owning an Alaskan Malamute means that free-running opportunities will be limited. As highlighted, this is a dog with a strong predatory drive and, no matter how well he is trained, this instinct will take over in certain circumstances.

However, this does not mean that you should neglect recall training – far from it. You need to establish a connection so your Mal respects you, and wants to come back to you, knowing that he will be rewarded for his co-operation.

Hopefully, you will have a reasonably large garden for your Malamute, so even in this confined situation, you will need a good recall. Malamute owners are skilled at finding safe areas for limited free running, but do seek advice before letting your dog off leash.

The breeder may have started this lesson, simply by calling the puppies to "Come" when it is a mealtime, or when they are moving from one place to another.

You can build on this when your puppy arrives in his new home, calling him to "Come" when he is in a confined space, such as the kitchen. This is a good place to build up a positive association with the verbal cue – particularly if you ask your puppy to "Come" to get his dinner!

The next stage is to transfer the lesson to the garden. Arm yourself with some treats, and wait until your puppy is distracted. Then call him, using a higher-pitched, excited tone of voice. At this stage, a puppy wants to be with you, so capitalize on this and keep practicing the verbal cue, and rewarding your puppy with a treat and lots of praise when he comes to you.

Coming back to you should always be a rewarding experience.

Now you are ready to introduce some distractions. Try calling him when someone else is in the garden, or wait a few minutes until he is investigating a really interesting scent. When he responds, make a really big fuss of him and give him some extra treats so he knows it is worth his while to come to you. If your puppy responds, immediately reward him with a treat.

If he is slow to come, run away a few steps and then call again, making yourself sound really exciting. Jump up and down, open your arms wide to welcome him; it doesn't matter how silly you look, he needs to see you as the most fun person in the world.

When you have a reliable recall in the garden, you can venture into the outside world, making sure you choose an area that has been tested as safe for Malamutes. Do not be too ambitious to begin with; try a recall in a quiet place with the minimum of distractions so you can be assured of success..

Do not make the mistake of only asking your dog to come at the end of his allotted exercise period. What is the incentive in coming back to you if all you do is clip on his leash, marking the end of his free time? Instead, call your dog at random times, giving him a treat and a stroke, and then letting him go free again. In this way, coming to you is always rewarding, and does not signal the end of his free run.

Stationary exercises

The Sit and Down are easy to teach, and mastering these exercises will be rewarding for both you and your Malamute.

Sit

The best method is to lure your Mal into position, and for this you can use a treat, a toy, or his food bowl.

- Hold the reward (a treat or food bowl) above his head. As he looks up, he will lower his hindquarters and go into a Sit.

- Practice this a few times and when your puppy understands what you are asking, introduce the verbal cue, "Sit".

- When your Malamute understands the exercise, he will respond to the verbal cue alone, and you will not need to reward him every time he sits. However, it is a good idea to give him a treat on a random basis when he co-operates, to keep him guessing!

Down

This is an important lesson, and can be a life-saver if an emergency arises and you need to bring your Malamute to an instant halt.

- You can start with your dog in a Sit or a Stand for this exercise. Stand or kneel in front of him and show him you have a treat in your hand. Hold the treat just in front of his nose and slowly lower it towards the ground, between his front legs.

- As your Mal follows the treat he will go down on his front legs and, in a few moments, his hindquarters will follow. Close your hand over the treat so he doesn't cheat and get the treat before he is in the correct position. As soon as he is in the Down, give him the treat and lots of praise.

- Keep practicing, and when your Malamute understands what you want, introduce the verbal cue "Down".

Control
exercises

These exercises are not the most exciting but they are useful in a variety of different situations. It also teaches your Alaskan Malamute that you are someone to be respected, and if he co-operates, he is always rewarded for making the right decision.

Wait

This exercise teaches your Malamute to "Wait" in position until you give the next command; it differs from the Stay exercise where he must stay where you have left him for a more prolonged period. The most useful application of "Wait" is when you are getting your dog out of the car and you need him to stay in position until you clip on his leash.

- Start with your puppy on the leash to give you a greater chance of success. Ask him to "Sit", and

stand in front him. Step back one pace, holding your hand, palm flat, facing him. Wait a second and then come back to stand in front of him. You can then reward him and release him with a word, such as "OK".

- Practice this a few times, waiting a little longer before you reward him, and then introduce the verbal cue "Wait".

- You can reinforce the lesson by using it in different situations, such as asking your Malamute to "Wait" before you put his food bowl down.

Stay

You need to differentiate this exercise from the Wait by using a different hand signal and a different verbal cue.

- Start with your Malamute in the Down, as he is most likely to be secure in this position. Stand by his side and then step forwards, with your hand held back, palm facing the dog.

- Step back, release him, and then reward him. Practice until your Mal understands the exercise and then introduce the verbal cue "Stay".

- Gradually increase the distance you can leave your puppy, and increase the challenge by walking around him – and even stepping over him – so that he learns he must "Stay" until you release him.

Leave

A response to this verbal cue means that your Malamute will learn to give up a toy on request, and it follows that he will give up anything when he is asked, which is very useful if he has hold of a forbidden object. You can also use it if you catch him red-handed raiding the bin, or digging up a prized plant in the garden.

- The Alaskan Malamute has a possessive side to his nature, and this can apply to food and to toys. It is, therefore, important that your puppy learns that if he gives up something, he will get a reward, which may be even better than he already has.

- The "Leave" command can be taught quite easily when you are first playing with your puppy. As you gently, take a toy from his mouth, introduce the verbal cue, "Leave", and then praise him.

- If he is reluctant, swap the toy for another toy or a treat. This will usually do the trick.

- Keep practising and rewarding your Mal so he thinks that "Leave" is always a good option.

Opportunities for Malamutes

The Alaskan Malamute has a strong work ethic and needs the opportunity to use his brain, as well as finding ways to expend his considerable energy. Above all, working with your dog will enhance the bond between you and will result in a more fulfilling, and respectful relationship.

Good Citizen Scheme

The Kennel Club Good Citizen Scheme was introduced to promote responsible dog ownership, and to teach dogs basic good manners. In the US there is one test; in the UK there are four award levels: Puppy Foundation, Bronze, Silver and Gold.

Facing page: Mixed breed teams of Siberian Huskies and Alaskan Malamutes may work together.

Exercises within the scheme include:

- Walking on leash

- Road walking

- Control at door/gate.

- Food manners

- Recall

- Stay

- Send to bed

- Emergency stop.

Canicross

This is a relatively new sport and it is tailor-made for fit owners who have dogs with high exercise requirements. Basically, it involves cross-country running attached to your dog. You will need some specialized equipment (a belt for you and a bungee-style line for your Malamute). Dogs must be 12 months old to compete, but you can start fitness training from around nine months and also teach all important instructions, such as "haw" (left), "gee" (right), "steady" and "Whoa!"

Rally O

If you do not want to get involved in the rigors of Competitive Obedience, you may find that a sport called Rally O is more to your liking.

This is loosely based on Obedience, and also has a few exercises borrowed from Agility when you get to the highest levels. Handler and dog must complete a course, in the designated order, which has a variety of different exercises that could number from 12 to 20. The course is timed and the team must complete within the time limit that is set, but there are no bonus marks for speed.

The great advantage of Rally O is that it is very relaxed, and anyone can compete; indeed, it has proved very popular for handlers with disabilities as they are able to work their dogs to a high standard and compete on equal terms.

Scootering/bikejoring

This involves your Malamute pulling you on a scooter or bicycle. As can be imagined, this involves a fair amount of training as the pace is fast and furious. Safety is of paramount importance to prevent the line getting caught in a wheel, so you will need expert help if you decide to take up this challenge.

Skijoring

You need the snow for this sport – as well as a great deal of skill. If you are proficient at skiing, you can train your Malamute to pull you while you are on skis. This is highly enjoyable for dog and handler, but a sport that must be reserved for those with the necessary expertise.

Mushing

This is a sport in which two or more Malamutes are attached to a sled. It can take place on snow, or in temperate climates a wheeled rig can be used. Races over varying distances are scheduled and it is highly competitive at the top level.

Weight pulling

This is a sport where a dog has to pull a loaded sled or cart over a short distance, which may be dirt, grass, carpet or snow. The dogs, which are mostly the sled dog breeds, and bull terrier types, wear a special harness which helps to distribute the weight and so reduce the risk of injury.

An Alaskan Malamute that is fit and trained can pull amazingly heavy weights; most can pull more than 450kg (1,000lb) with 900-1,360kg (2-3,000lb) being top weights in competition. Most dogs can pull more on carpet than on snow.

This sport was invented in the USA but it is now proving popular elsewhere, with sled dog organisations running their own competitions.

Agility

In this sport, the dog completes an obstacle course under the guidance of his owner. You need a good element of control, as the dog completes the course off the leash.

In competition, each dog completes the course individually and is assessed on both time and accuracy. The dog that completes the course with the fewest faults, in the fastest time, wins the class. The obstacles include an A-frame, a dog-walk, weaving poles, a seesaw, tunnels, and jumps.

Showing

Exhibiting a dog in the show ring may look simple but, in fact, it entails a lot of training and preparation. Your Malamute needs to remain calm in the busy show atmosphere, so you need to work on his socialization, and then take him to ringcraft classes so you both learn what is required in the ring. Your Malamute will be subjected to a detailed 'hands on' examination by the judge; he will need to stand still in a show pose and will also need to move on a loose leash so the judge can assess his gait.

Showing at the top level is highly addictive, so watch out – once you start, you will never have a free date in your diary!

Health care

We are fortunate that the Alaskan Malamute is a healthy dog and, with good routine care, a well-balanced diet, and sufficient exercise, most will experience few health problems.

However, it is your responsibility to put a program of preventative health care in place – and this should start from the moment your puppy, or older dog, arrives in his new home.

Vaccinations

Dogs are subject to a number of contagious diseases. In the old days, these were killers, and resulted in heartbreak for many owners. Vaccinations have now been developed, and the occurrence of the major infectious diseases is now very rare. However, this will only remain the case if all pet owners follow a strict policy of vaccinating their dogs.

There are vaccinations available for the following diseases:

Adenovirus: (Canine Adenovirus): This affects the liver; affected dogs have a classic 'blue eye'.

Distemper: A viral disease which causes chest and gastro-intestinal damage. The brain may also be affected, leading to fits and paralysis.

Parvovirus: Causes severe gastro enteritis, and most commonly affects puppies.

Leptospirosis: This bacterial disease is carried by rats and affects many mammals, including humans. It causes liver and kidney damage.

Rabies: A virus that affects the nervous system and is invariably fatal. The first signs are abnormal behavior, when the infected dog may bite another animal or a person. Paralysis and death follow. Vaccination is compulsory in most countries. In the UK, dogs traveling overseas must be vaccinated.

Kennel Cough: There are several strains of kennel cough, but they all result in a harsh, dry, cough. This disease is rarely fatal; in fact most dogs make a good recovery within a matter of weeks and show few signs of ill health while they are affected. However, kennel cough is highly infectious among dogs that live together so, for this reason, most boarding kennels will insist that your dog is protected by the vaccine, which is given as nose drops.

Lyme disease: This is a bacterial disease transmitted by ticks (see page 166). The first signs are limping, but the heart, kidneys and nervous system can also be affected. The ticks that transmit the disease occur in specific regions, such as the north-east states of the USA, some of the southern states, California and the upper Mississippi region. Lyme disease is still rare in the UK so vaccinations are not routinely offered.

Vaccination program

In the USA, the American Animal Hospital Association advises vaccination for core diseases, which they list as: distemper, adenovirus, parvovirus and rabies. The requirement for vaccinating for non-core diseases – leptospriosis, lyme disease and kennel cough – should be assessed depending on a dog's individual risk and his likely exposure to the disease.

In the UK, vaccinations are routinely given for distemper, adenovirus, leptospirosis and parvovirus.

In most cases, a puppy will start his vaccinations at around eight weeks of age, with the second part given a fortnight later. However, this does vary depending on the individual policy of veterinary practices, and the incidence of disease in your area.

You should also talk to your vet about whether to give annual booster vaccinations. This depends on an individual dog's levels of immunity, and how long a particular vaccine remains effective.

Parasites

No matter how well you look after your Alaskan Malamute, you will have to accept that parasites – internal and external – are ever present, and you need to take preventative action.

Internal parasites: As the name suggests, these parasites live inside your dog. Most will find a home in the digestive tract, but there is also a parasite that lives in the heart. If infestation is unchecked, a dog's health will be severely jeopardized, but routine preventative treatment is simple and effective.

External parasites: These parasites live on your dog's body – in his skin and fur, and sometimes in his ears.

Roundworm

This is found in the small intestine, and signs of infestation will be a poor coat, a pot belly, diarrhoea and lethargy. Pregnant mothers should be treated,

but it is almost inevitable that parasites will be passed on to the puppies. For this reason, a breeder will start a worming program, which you will need to continue. Ask your vet for advice on treatment, which will need to continue throughout your dog's life.

Tapeworm

Infection occurs when fleas and lice are ingested; the adult worm takes up residence in the small intestine, releasing mobile segments (which contain eggs) that can be seen in a dog's feces as small rice-like grains. The only other obvious sign of infestation is irritation of the anus. Again, routine preventative treatment is required throughout your Malamute's life.

Heartworm

This parasite is transmitted by mosquitoes, and so will only occur where these insects thrive. A warm environment is needed for the parasite to develop, so it is more likely to be present in areas with a warm, humid climate. However, it is found in all parts of the USA, although its prevalence does vary. At present, heartworm is rarely seen in the UK.

Heartworm live in the right side of the heart. Larvae can grow up to 35cm (14in) in length. A dog with heartworm is at severe risk from heart failure, so preventative treatment, as advised by your vet, is essential. Dogs living in the USA should have regular blood tests to check for the presence of infection.

Lungworm

Lungworm, or *Angiostrongylus vasorum*, is a parasite that lives in the heart and major blood vessels supplying the lungs. It can cause many problems, such as breathing difficulties, blood-clotting problems, sickness and diarrhoea, seizures, and can even be fatal. The parasite is carried by slugs and snails, and the dog becomes infected when ingesting these, often accidentally when rummaging through undergrowth. Lungworm is not common, but it is on the increase and a responsible owner should be aware of it. Fortunately, it is easily preventable and even affected dogs usually make a full recovery if treated early enough. Your vet will be able to advise you on the risks in your area and what form of treatment may be required.

Fleas

A dog may carry dog fleas, cat fleas, and even human fleas. The flea stays on the dog only long enough to have a blood meal and to breed, but its presence will result in itching and scratching. If your dog has an allergy to fleas – which is usually a reaction to the flea's saliva – he will scratch himself until he is raw.

Spot-on treatment, which should be administered on a routine basis, is easy to use and highly effective on all types of fleas. You can also treat your dog with a spray or with insecticidal shampoo. Bear in mind that the whole environment your dog lives in will need to be sprayed, and all other pets living in your home will also need to be treated.

How to detect fleas

You may suspect your dog has fleas, but how can you be sure? There are two methods to try.

Run a fine comb through your dog's coat, and see if you can detect the presence of fleas on the skin, or clinging to the comb. Alternatively, sit your dog on white paper and rub his back. This will dislodge feces from the fleas, which will be visible as small brown specks. To double check, shake the specks on to some damp cotton (cotton-wool). Flea feces consists of the dried blood taken from the host, so if the specks turn a lighter shade of red, you know your dog has fleas.

Ticks

These are blood-sucking parasites most frequently found in rural /areas where sheep or deer are present. The main danger is their ability to pass lyme disease to both dogs and humans. Lyme disease is prevalent in some areas of the USA (see page 161), although it is still rare in the UK. The treatment you give your dog for fleas generally works for ticks, but you should discuss the best product to use with your vet.

How to remove a tick

If you spot a tick on your dog, do not try to pluck it off as you risk leaving the hard mouth parts embedded in his skin. The best way to remove a tick is to use a fine pair of tweezers, or you can buy a tick remover. Grasp the tick head firmly and then pull the tick straight out from the skin. If you are using a tick remover, check the instructions, as some recommend a circular twist when pulling. When you have removed the tick, clean the area with mild soap and water.

Ear mites

These parasites live in the outer ear canal. The signs of infestation are a brown, waxy discharge, and your dog will continually shake his head and scratch his ear. If you suspect your Malamute has ear mites, a visit to the vet will be needed so that medicated ear drops can be prescribed.

Fur mites

These small, white parasites are visible to the naked eye and are often referred to as 'walking dandruff'. They cause a scurfy coat and mild itchiness. However, they are zoonotic – transferable to humans – so prompt treatment with an insecticide prescribed by your vet is essential.

Harvest mites

These are picked up from the undergrowth, and can be seen as a bright orange patch on the webbing between the toes, although this can be found elsewhere on the body, such as on the ear flaps. Treatment is effective with the appropriate insecticide.

Skin mites

There are two types of parasite that burrow into a dog's skin. *Demodex canis* is transferred from a mother to her pups while they are feeding. Treatment is with a topical preparation, and sometimes antibiotics are needed.

The other skin mite, *Sarcoptes scabiei*, causes intense itching and hair loss. It is highly contagious, so all dogs in a household will need to be treated, which involves repeated bathing with a medicated shampoo.

Common
ailments

As with all living animals, dogs can be affected by a variety of ailments. Most can be treated effectively after consulting with your vet, who will prescribe appropriate medication and will advise you on how to care for your dog's needs.

Here are some of the more common problems that could affect your Alaskan Malamute, with advice on how to deal with them.

Anal glands

These are two small sacs on either side of the anus, which produce a dark-brown secretion that dogs use when they mark their territory. The anal glands should empty every time a dog defecates but if they become blocked or impacted, a dog will experience increasing discomfort. He may nibble at his rear end, or 'scoot' his bottom along the ground to relieve the irritation.

Treatment involves a trip to the vet, where the glands can be emptied manually. It is important to do this without delay or infection may occur.

Dental problems

Good dental hygiene will do much to minimize gum infection and tooth decay. If tartar accumulates to the extent that you cannot remove it by brushing, the vet will need to intervene. In a situation such as this, an anesthetic will need to be administered so the tartar can be removed manually.

Diarrhoea

There are many reasons why a dog has diarrhoea, but most commonly it is the result of scavenging, a sudden change of diet, or an adverse reaction to a particular type of food.

If your dog is suffering from diarrhoea, the first step is to withdraw food for a day. It is important that he does not dehydrate, so make sure that fresh drinking water is available. However, drinking too much can increase the diarrhoea, which may be accompanied with vomiting, so limit how much he drinks at any one time.

After allowing the stomach to rest, feed a bland diet, such as white fish or chicken with boiled rice, for a few days. In most cases, your dog's motions will return to normal and you can resume usual feeding, although this should be done gradually.

However, if this fails to work and the diarrhoea

persists for more than a few days, you should consult you vet. Your dog may have an infection which needs to be treated with antibiotics, or the diarrhoea may indicate some other problem which needs expert diagnosis.

Ear infections

The Alaskan Malamute has erect ears, which allows air to circulate freely, thereby minimizing the risk of ear infections.

A healthy ear is clean with no sign of redness or inflammation, and no evidence of a waxy brown discharge or a foul odor. If you see your dog scratching his ear, shaking his head, or holding one ear at an odd angle, you will need to consult your vet.

The most likely causes are ear mites, an infection, or there may a foreign body, such as a grass seed, trapped in the ear.

Depending on the cause, treatment is with medicated ear drops, possibly containing antibiotics. If a foreign body is suspected, the vet will need to carry our further investigation.

Eye problems

The Malamute has almond-shaped eyes, set obliquely in the skull. They do not bulge, which would make them vulnerable to injury.

If your Malamute's eyes look red and sore, he may be suffering from conjunctivitis. This may, or may not be accompanied with a watery or a crusty discharge. Conjunctivitis can be caused by a bacterial or viral infection, it could be the result of an injury, or it could be an adverse reaction to pollen.

You will need to consult your vet for a correct diagnosis, but in the case of an infection, treatment with medicated eye drops is effective.

Conjunctivitis may also be the first sign of more serious inherited eye problems (see page 184).

In some instances, a dog may suffer from dry, itchy eye, which your dog may further injure through scratching. This condition, known as keratoconjunctivitis sicca, may be inherited.

Foreign bodies

In the home, puppies – and some older dogs – cannot resist chewing anything that looks interesting. The toys you choose for your dog should be suitably robust to withstand damage, but children's toys can be irresistible. Some dogs will chew – and swallow – anything from socks, tights, and any other items from the laundry basket to golf balls and stones from the garden. Obviously, these items are indigestible and could cause an obstruction in your dog's intestine, which is potentially lethal.

The signs to look for are vomiting, and a tucked up posture. The dog will often be restless and will look as though he is in pain.

In this situation, you must take your dog to the vet without delay as surgery will be needed to remove the obstruction.

Heatstroke

The Malamute's head structure is without exaggeration, which means that he has a straightforward respiratory system.

However, this is a dog that was bred to withstand the harsh climate of the Nordic lands so, consequently, many Malamutes have a low tolerance to heat. If the weather is warm, make sure your Malamute always has access to shady areas, and wait for a cooler part of the day before going for a walk. Be extra careful if you leave your Malamute in the car, as the temperature can rise dramatically - even on a cloudy day. Heatstroke can happen very rapidly, and unless you are able lower your dog's temperature, it can be fatal.

If your Malamute appears to be suffering from heatstroke, lie him flat and work at lowering his temperature by spraying him with cool water and covering him with wet towels. As soon as he has made some recovery, take him to the vet where cold intravenous fluids can be administered.

Lameness/limping

There are a wide variety of reasons why a dog can go lame, from a simple muscle strain, to a fracture, ligament damage, or more complex problems with the joints. If you are concerned about your dog, do not delay in seeking help.

As your Malamute becomes more elderly, he may suffer from arthritis, which you will see as general stiffness, particularly when he gets up after resting. It will help if you ensure his bed is in a warm draft-free location, and if your Malamute gets wet after exercise, you must dry him thoroughly.

If you Malamute seems to be in pain, consult your vet who will be able to help with pain relief medication.

Skin problems

If your dog is scratching or nibbling at his skin, first check he is free from fleas (see page 165). There are other external parasites which cause itching and hair loss, but you will need a vet to help you find the culprit.

An allergic reaction can cause major skin problems, but it can be quite an undertaking to find the cause of the allergy. You will need to follow your vet's advice, which often requires eliminating specific ingredients from the diet, as well as looking at environmental factors.

The Alaskan Malamute is predisposed to a condition known as zinc-responsive dermatosis (see page 188), and there is a tendency to suffer from moist eczema, commonly referred to as 'hot spots' (see page 186).

Breed-specific disorders

Like all pedigree dogs, the Alaskan Malamute does have a few breed-related disorders. If diagnosed with any of the diseases listed below, it is important to remember that they can affect offspring, so breeding from affected dogs should be discouraged.

There are now recognised screening tests to enable breeders to check for affected individuals and hence reduce the prevalence of these diseases within the breed.

DNA testing is also becoming more widely available, and as research into the different genetic diseases progresses, more DNA tests are being developed.

Gastric dilation/volvulus

This condition, commonly known as bloat or gastric torsion, is where the stomach swells visibly (dilatation) and then rotates (volvulus), so that the exit into the small intestine becomes blocked, preventing food from leaving. This results in stomach pain and a bloated abdomen. It is a severe, life-threatening condition that requires immediate veterinary attention (usually surgery) to decompress and return the stomach to its normal position.

There appear to be several risk factors causing the development of GDV and by taking the following precautions, you can reduce the risk.

- Feed two smaller meals per day instead one large one.

- Do not allow the dog to drink a large volume of water at one time.

- Do not feed immediately before or after strenuous exercise – wait at least two hours.

Diabetes mellitus

This involves a disruption of the body's ability to use sugar and carbohydrates. In some forms insulin, the hormone which controls the uptake of sugar into the body, is not produced; in other forms insulin is produced but the body tissues fail to respond.

The typical signs are increased eating, drinking and urination, often accompanied by weight loss. In severe cases, the condition may be apparent by six months of age, but it is more likely to develop in middle age. Insulin will need to be administered in order to normalise blood glucose levels.

Eye disorders

Alaskan Malamutes may be affected by eye disorders. Testing is carried out by the Canine Eye Registration Foundation in the US; in the UK there is a combined scheme run by the British Veterinary Association, the Kennel Club and the International Sheep Dog Society.

Cataracts

Cataracts are an opacification of the lens that tends to occur in older dogs. There are varying degrees of severity; a complete cataract in each eye will result in complete blindness, whereas small, non progressive cataracts have little effect on eyesight. Surgery is usually an effective form of treatment.

The Canine Eye Registration Foundation (CERF), in the US, recommends annual eye testing, and affected dogs should not be bred from.

Glaucoma

This is the result of increased fluid pressure within the eye. It can cause permanent damage, and if untreated, blindness may result. The condition, which is very painful, can deteriorate gradually, or there may be a sudden, acute episode resulting is total loss of vision within 24 hours.

Breeding stock should be screened for the condition;

affected dogs and their close relatives should not be bred from.

Hip dysplasia (HD)

This is where the ball-and-socket joint of the hip develops incorrectly, so that the head of the femur (ball) and the acetabulum of the pelvis (socket) do not fit snugly. This causes pain in the joint and may be seen as lameness in dogs as young as five months old with deterioration into severe arthritis over time.

In the US, hip scoring is carried out by the Orthopaedic Foundation for Animals. X-rays are submitted when a dog is two years old, categorised as Normal (Excellent, Good, Fair), Borderline, and Dysplastic (Mild, Moderate, Severe). The hip grades of Excellent, Good and Fair are within normal limits and are given OFA numbers.

In the UK, the minimum age for the hips to be assessed by X-ray is 12 months. Each hip can score from a possible perfect 0 to a deformed 53. Both left and right scores are added together to give the total hip score.

Hot spots

The Alaskan Malamute has a tendency to suffer from moist eczema, more commonly known as hot spots. This is a skin condition caused by bacteria which thrive in a slightly most environment, such as when a Mal gets wet during exercise, or has not been thoroughly dried after a bath. The skin becomes itchy and, as the dog scratches, it becomes red and sore.

Hot spots can be treated with topical medication from the vet, but you may need to trim the affected area to allow it to dry out completely.

Osteochondysplasia (Skeletal Dwarfism)

As a dog grows and develops, cartilage turns in to bone. When there are irregularities in this process skeletal dwarfism results. In most cases, the limbs are short relative to the body length, although sometimes the vertebrae are affected, which means the body is abnormally short.

Mildly affected dogs will not suffer any clinical problems, but in severe cases, the limbs may be

deformed, causing lameness, intolerance to exercise and sometimes major debilitation. Affected dogs are more likely to develop arthritis and joint pain.

There is no specific treatment. Affected dogs, their parents, and their siblings should be eliminated from breeding programs.

Zinc-responsive dermatosis

This is a skin condition that affects the Nordic breeds – the Alaskan Malamute, the Siberian Husky and the Samoyed. It is caused by a genetic abnormality which makes it difficult for them to retain zinc.

Signs are usually seen around puberty with redness, scaling and crustiness on the muzzle and around the eyes, often accompanied by hair loss. The pads of the feet and the area around the anus may also be affected. In some cases the dog will itch and chew at his feet.

Diagnosis is by skin biopsy, and treatment is by zinc supplementation, which will need to be continued throughout a dog's life. If left untreated, the whole immune system may be compromised.

Summing up

It may concern the pet owner to find about health problems that may affect their dog. But it is important to bear in mind that acquiring some basic knowledge is an asset, as it will allow you to spot signs of trouble at an early stage. Early diagnosis is very often the means to the most effective treatment.

Fortunately, the Alaskan Malamute is a generally healthy and disease-free dog with his only visits to the vet being annual check-ups. In most cases, owners can look forward to enjoying many happy years with this outstanding companion.

Useful addresses

Please contact your Kennel Club to obtain contact information about breed clubs in your area.

UK

The Kennel Club (UK)
1 Clarges Street London, W1J 8AB
Telephone: 0870 606 6750
Fax: 0207 518 1058
Web: www.thekennelclub.org.uk

USA

American Kennel Club (AKC)
5580 Centerview Drive, Raleigh, NC 27606.
Telephone: 919 233 9767
Fax: 919 233 3627
Email: info@akc.org
Web: www.akc.org

United Kennel Club (UKC)
100 E Kilgore Rd, Kalamazoo,
MI 49002-5584, USA.
Tel: 269 343 9020
Fax: 269 343 7037
Web:www.ukcdogs.com/

Australia

Australian National Kennel Council (ANKC)
The Australian National Kennel Council is the administrative body for pure breed canine affairs in Australia. It does not, however, deal directly with dog exhibitors, breeders or judges. For information pertaining to breeders, clubs or shows, please contact the relevant State or Territory Body.

International

Fédération Cynologique Internationalé (FCI)
Place Albert 1er, 13, B-6530 Thuin, Belgium.
Tel: +32 71 59.12.38
Fax: +32 71 59.22.29
Web: www.fci.be/

Training and behavior
UK

Association of Pet Dog Trainers
Telephone: 01285 810811
Web: http://www.apdt.co.uk

Canine Behaviour
Association of Pet Behaviour Counsellors
Telephone: 01386 751151
Web: http://www.apbc.org.uk/

USA

Association of Pet Dog Trainers
Tel: 1 800 738 3647
Web: www.apdt.com/

American College of Veterinary Behaviorists
Web: http://dacvb.org/

American Veterinary Society of Animal Behavior
Web: www.avsabonline.org/

Australia

APDT Australia Inc
Web: www.apdt.com.au

For details of regional behaviorists, contact the relevant State or Territory Controlling Body.

Activities

UK

Agility Club
http://www.agilityclub.co.uk/

British Flyball Association
Telephone: 01628 829623
Web: http://www.flyball.org.uk/

USA

North American Dog Agility Council
Web: www.nadac.com/

North American Flyball Association, Inc.
Tel/Fax: 800 318 6312
Web: www.flyball.org/

Australia

Agility Dog Association of Australia
Tel: 0423 138 914
Web: www.adaa.com.au/

NADAC Australia
Web: www.nadacaustralia.com/

Australian Flyball Association
Tel: 0407 337 939
Web: www.flyball.org.au/

International

World Canine Freestyle Organisation
Tel: (718) 332-8336
Web: www.worldcaninefreestyle.org

Health

UK

British Small Animal Veterinary Association
Tel: 01452 726700
Web: http://www.bsava.com/

Royal College of Veterinary Surgeons
Tel: 0207 222 2001
Web: www.rcvs.org.uk

www.dogbooksonline.co.uk/healthcare/

Alternative Veterinary Medicine Centre
Tel: 01367 710324
Web: www.alternativevet.org/

USA

American Veterinary Medical Association
Tel: 800 248 2862
Web: www.avma.org

American College of Veterinary Surgeons
Tel: 301 916 0200
Toll Free: 877 217 2287
Web: www.acvs.org/

Canine Eye Registration Foundation
The Veterinary Medical DataBases
1717 Philo Rd, PO Box 3007,
Urbana, IL 61803-3007
Tel: 217-693-4800
Fax: 217-693-4801
Web: http://www.vmdb.org/cerf.html

Orthopaedic Foundation of Animals
2300 E Nifong Boulevard
Columbia, Missouri, 65201-3806
Tel: 573 442-0418
Fax: 573 875-5073
Web: http://www.offa.org/

American Holistic Veterinary Medical
Association
Tel: 410 569 0795
Web: www.ahvma.org/

Australia

Australian Small Animal Veterinary
Association
Tel: 02 9431 5090
Web: www.asava.com.au

Australian Veterinary Association
Tel: 02 9431 5000
Web: www.ava.com.au

Australian College Veterinary Scientists
Tel: 07 3423 2016
Web: http://acvsc.org.au

Australian Holistic Vets
Web: www.ahv.com.au/